W9-AUY-165

First Facts®

First Cookbooks

# A Monster COOKBOOK

## Simple Recipes for Kids

by Sarah L. Schuette

CAPSTONE PRESS
a capstone imprint

First Facts is published by Capstone Press,
151 Good Counsel Drive, P.O. Box 669, Mankato, Minnesota 56002.
www.capstonepub.com

Books published by Capstone Press are manufactured with paper
containing at least 10 percent post-consumer waste.

*Library of Congress Cataloging-in-Publication Data*
Schuette, Sarah L., 1976–
  A monster cookbook : simple recipes for kids / by Sarah L. Schuette.
    p. cm.—(First facts. First cookbooks)
  Summary: "Provides instructions and close-up step photos for making a variety of simple snacks and
drinks with a monster theme"—Provided by publisher.
  Includes bibliographical references and index.
  ISBN 978-1-4296-5377-0 (library binding)
  1.  Cooking—Juvenile literature.  I. Title. II. Series.

  TX652.5.S3436 2011
  641.5'123—dc22

                              2010028140

**Editorial Credits**

Lori Shores, editor; Juliette Peters, designer; Sarah Schuette, photo stylist; Marcy Morin, studio scheduler;
    Laura Manthe, production specialist

**Photo Credits**

All photos by Capstone Studio/Karon Dubke

The author dedicates this book to her goddaughter, Muriel Hilgers.

Printed in the United States of America in North Mankato, Minnesota.
092010
005933CGS11

# Table of Contents

# Hungry Monsters

Sometimes when you're really hungry, your belly sounds like a growling monster. What can you do? Stomp into the kitchen and make yourself a snack. There are plenty of frightfully good recipes to try.

First you'll need a plan of attack. Read over the recipes. Dig through the cupboards for what you need. Have questions? Ask a grownup monster.

Monsters are dirty. But you know better! Make sure to wash your hands before you begin. And don't forget to clean up after yourself. The other monsters in your family will thank you.

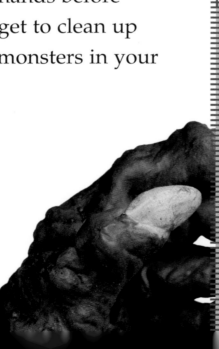

| Metric Conversion Chart | |
| --- | --- |
| **United States** | **Metric** |
| ¼ teaspoon | 1.2 mL |
| ½ teaspoon | 2.5 mL |
| 1 teaspoon | 5 mL |
| 1 tablespoon | 15 mL |
| ¼ cup | 60 mL |
| ⅓ cup | 80 mL |
| ½ cup | 120 mL |
| ⅔ cup | 160 mL |
| ¾ cup | 175 mL |
| 1 cup | 240 mL |
| 1 ounce | 30 gms |

# Tools

Monsters aren't picky. They usually use whatever tools they can find. Gather the tools you need before you begin.

**baking sheet**—a flat, metal pan used for baking foods

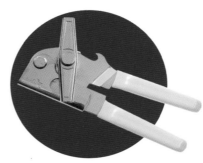

**can opener**—a tool used to open metal cans

**liquid measuring cup**—a glass or plastic measuring cup with a spout for pouring

**measuring cups**—round, flat cups with handles used for measuring dry ingredients

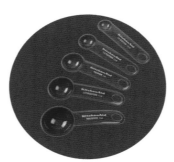

**measuring spoons**—spoons with small deep scoops used to measure both wet and dry ingredients

**microwave-safe bowl**—a non-metal bowl used to heat ingredients in a microwave oven

**mixing bowl**—a sturdy bowl used for mixing ingredients

**oven mitt**—a large mitten made from heavy fabric used to protect hands when removing hot pans from the oven

**rubber scraper**—a kitchen tool with a rubber paddle on one end

# Techniques

**strainer**—a bowl-shaped tool with holes in the sides and bottom

**drain**—to remove the liquid from something

**drizzle**—to let a liquid fall in small drops

**fold**—to mix ingredients gently by lifting a mixture up and over itself

**measure**—to take a specific amount of something

**roll**—to turn over and over in your hands to form a ball shape

**slice**—to cut into thin pieces

**sprinkle**—to scatter in small drops or bits

**stir**—to mix something by moving a spoon around in it

# Cyclops Eyes

A **cyclops** is a giant monster with one huge eye. These eyes are big on flavor. You'll want to eat more than one!

**Makes 24 2-inch eyes**

**Ingredients:**
- 1 cup peanut butter
- 1 cup honey
- 1 cup crispy rice cereal
- 1 cup powdered milk

**Tools:**
- measuring cup
- mixing bowl
- spoon
- baking sheet
- wax paper

8

**1** Measure and add peanut butter, honey, cereal, and powdered milk to a mixing bowl.

**2** Use a spoon to stir the mixture.

**3** Roll some of the mixture into a 2-inch ball with your hands. Lay the ball on a baking sheet covered with wax paper. Repeat.

**4** Place the baking sheet in the refrigerator for one hour.

**TIP** Use a round piece of candy to make this treat look more like an eye. Just press the candy into the middle of the ball.

# Swampy S'mores

Outside their **swampy** homes, **ogres** love roasting anything, even marshmallows. You can make your own s'mores without even going outside.

**Makes 1 s'more**

Ingredients:
- 2 graham cracker squares
- 1 chocolate candy bar square
- 1 large marshmallow

Tools:
- plate
- microwave

**1** Place one graham cracker square on a plate.

**2** Put a chocolate square on top of the graham cracker.

**3** Put a marshmallow on top of the chocolate.

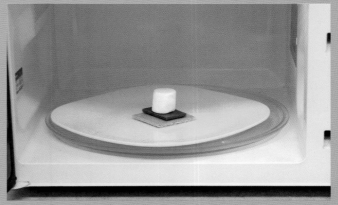

**4** Have an adult help you heat the s'more in the microwave for 30 seconds.

**5** Top the gooey marshmallow with another graham cracker square and press down.

**TIP** For a fruity twist, replace the marshmallow with a few slices of banana.

# King Kong Krunch

On Skull Island, King Kong crunched on bones. But this crunchy snack tastes much better. Your friends will want to climb the Empire State Building to get more.

**Makes 4 servings**

### Ingredients:
- 1 cup corn cereal squares
- 1 cup pretzel sticks
- 1 bag microwave popcorn
- 1 packet taco seasoning
- ½ stick butter
- grated Parmesan cheese

### Tools:
- measuring cups
- large bowl
- microwave
- spoon
- microwave-safe bowl

**1** Measure and pour cereal and pretzels into a large bowl.

**2** Have an adult help you make the microwave popcorn. Add popcorn to the bowl.

**3** Sprinkle taco seasoning on the mixture. Stir gently to mix.

**4** Place butter in a microwave-safe bowl. Have an adult help you melt the butter in the microwave.

**5** Use a spoon to drizzle melted butter over all ingredients in the large bowl.

**6** Sprinkle with grated Parmesan cheese to taste. Stir gently to coat evenly.

# Godzilla Salad

Godzilla is a green movie star that never eats in his movies. No wonder he's hungry! If you made him this salad, he'd gobble it up.

**Makes 4 servings**

**Ingredients:**

- 1 package instant pistachio pudding, 3.4 ounces
- 1 container cottage cheese, 12 ounces
- 1 can pineapple tidbits, 20 ounces
- 2 cups whipped topping

**Tools:**

- large bowl
- spoon
- can opener
- strainer
- measuring cups
- rubber scraper

**1** Pour dry pudding mix and cottage cheese into a large bowl.

**2** Use a spoon to stir the ingredients together.

**3** Have an adult help you open the can of pineapple. Use a strainer to drain liquid from pineapple.

**4** Add pineapple to bowl. Stir ingredients together.

**5** Measure and add whipped topping. Use a rubber scraper to fold whipped topping into pineapple mixture.

**TIP**

If you're wild about fruit, add a can of fruit cocktail to your salad. Just drain the liquid first.

# Giant Squid Sandwich

Giant **squids** are monsterlike animals that swim deep in the ocean. They use eight arms and two long **tentacles** to grab fish. Enjoy this "squid" sandwich at home, far from a real squid's grasp.

**Makes 1 sandwich**

**Ingredients:**
- 1 hot dog
- 1 whole wheat tortilla
- 1 slice American cheese

**Tools:**
- 2 plates
- butter knife
- microwave
- toothpick

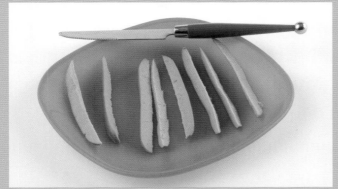

**1** Place a hot dog on a plate. Have an adult help you slice the hot dog into eight strips with a butter knife.

**2** Have the adult help you microwave the hot dog pieces for one minute.

**3** Place a tortilla on another plate. Tear a slice of cheese in half and place on the tortilla.

**4** Put the hot dog pieces on top of the cheese.

**5** Fold up the tortilla and secure with a toothpick. Have an adult help you microwave the sandwich for 30 seconds.

## TIP

Dip your giant squid sandwich into ketchup or mustard.

# Nessie's Breakfast

Stories say that a monster named Nessie swims in a deep lake in Scotland. But the water in **Loch** Ness is so dark, it's like trying to see through oatmeal! You'll have an easier time getting through this oatmeal.

**Makes 1 serving**

**Ingredients:**
- ½ cup quick-cook oatmeal
- ¼ cup dried cranberries
- ¾ cup water
- 1 teaspoon honey

**Tools:**
- measuring cups
- microwave-safe bowl
- liquid measuring cup
- microwave
- oven mitts
- spoon
- measuring spoons

**TIP** Nessie might eat the same thing day after day, but you don't have to. Next time, add cinnamon, dried fruits, or jelly to your oatmeal.

18

**1** Measure oatmeal and pour into a microwave-safe bowl.

**2** Measure and add cranberries.

**3** Use a liquid measuring cup to measure and add water.

**4** Have an adult help you microwave the oatmeal for two minutes.

**5** Use oven mitts to take bowl out of microwave. Stir and let cool for one minute.

**6** Measure honey. Use measuring spoon to drizzle honey over the oatmeal.

# Bigfoot's Boogers

Bigfoot probably snacks on anything he finds in the forest. But even he wouldn't eat boogers! If you found this snack in the forest, you might think Bigfoot left it behind.

**Makes 4 servings**

### Ingredients:
- 1 fresh broccoli crown, cut into pieces
- 1 can spray cheese, 8 ounces
- ½ cup bacon bits

### Tools:
- 2 bowls
- measuring cups
- spoon

**1** Wash broccoli pieces and place in a bowl.

**2** Top each broccoli piece with cheese. Set the broccoli pieces in a shallow bowl.

**3** Measure bacon bits. Use a spoon to sprinkle bacon bits over the cheese.

**TIP** Instead of using cheese, try making a dipping sauce. Just add green food coloring and bacon bits to ¼ cup sour cream.

# Glossary

**cyclops** (SY-klahps)—in Greek mythology, a giant with one eye in the middle of its forehead

**loch** (LAHK)—the Scottish word for lake; Loch Ness is a large freshwater lake in Scotland

**ogre** (OH-gur)—a fierce, cruel giant or monster in fairy tales and folktales

**squid** (SKWID)—a sea animal with a long, soft body, eight arms, and two tentacles

**swampy** (SWAHMP-ee)—swamplike; swamps are areas of wet, spongy ground

**tentacle** (TEN-tuh-kuhl)—a long, armlike body part

# Read More

**Wilkes, Angela.** *First Cooking Activity Book.* London: Dorling Kindersley, 2008.

**Williams, Zac.** *Little Monsters Cookbook: Recipes and Photographs.* Layton, Utah: Gibbs Smith, 2010.

# Internet Sites

FactHound offers a safe, fun way to find Internet sites related to this book. All of the sites on FactHound have been researched by our staff.

Here's all you do:

Visit *www.facthound.com*

Type in this code: 9781429653770

Super-cool stuff! Check out projects, games and lots more at www.capstonekids.com

# Index